To my son.

Copyright © 2022 Vivienne Lee

All rights reserved. No part of this book may be reproduced or used in any manner without the prior written permission of the cop yright owner, except for the use of brief quotations in a book review.

Author: Vivienne Lee
Publisher: Simon Lee
ISBN 978-1-3999-4577-6
Printed in England

FEAR NOT
THE SPIRITUAL
TRUTH

Vivienne Lee

A Coruña, Galicia (Spain)
2022

Introduction

Hi everyone.

In this book I have given a true account of all the paranormal experiences I have been through in the hopes that in some way my story will help others not to fear dying and at the same time it's vital we defend our democratic rights.

I would also like to give a warning to anyone who is thinking about meditation on ones own. If you have no previous experience, then always be guided by a professional. In my particular case I was very afraid, but now I realise that it had to be that way. I had to go through all these experiences because if I hadn't I wouldn't have been able to write this book. Meditating for me now is a "must" in my daily routine. It brings me a feeling of just being free, and nothing seems important. It just makes me feel calm and peaceful and has brought me closer to God and the Universe.

I know that everyone suffers in one way or another, I don't think that many escape from sad memories of losing loved ones. Broken marriages, financial difficulties, how to bring up the kids... It's not easy for anyone. We all do the best we can even if it's not the right way. Who knows? We can't judge anyone. We are human beings, and we all make mistakes. Sometimes you know as well as I do that we make the same mistake over and over again.

It's our own individual journey and we do the best we can whether it goes right or wrong. I imagine that some of our previous lives have been the same, but we just change the roles we play. It's all about learning, and maybe in our previous lives we forget what we came here to do and have to come back again. In my opinion as long as you know who you are to yourself, it doesn't really matter what other people think of you. If everyone got on with their own lives instead of worrying about others, I think the world would be a better place to live in.

I am no Saint. I have done things I shouldn't have done, but I can only ask for forgiveness because it cannot be erased. It's the past and nothing can change that. It's just as easy to be nice as to be nasty. It's just as easy to love instead of hate. Let's try it. We have nothing to lose and everything to gain. God bless you whatever colour you are, whatever creed or religion, we are all a part of this wonderful community and have a bond between us. We are one!

Be brave my little ones, fear not the Spiritual truth. I beg and pray that love and peace will reign on Mother Earth, she deserves love and attention, bless her. Let's shed no more blood. She cherishes our love, and so do I cherish yours. Be kind, help others who need to be heard and most of all thank God for existing.

I LOVE YOU ALL AND SEND YOU
A KISS OF LOVE AND LIGHT FOR
THE FUTURE OF OUR PLANET

GOD BLESS

1
UNANSWERED QUESTIONS

When I was a little girl, I often laid in bed and asked myself if I was really me? Who was I? Where had I come from?

I asked myself these questions over and over again and then started to feel weird and thought why was I asking myself these questions. I even asked if I was really alive or was I just dreaming. Strange questions for a child I suppose, but I never got the answers.

We were a big family, nine of us, although Mum and Dad passed over some years ago, so now there are seven of us, six daughters and one son.

Can you imagine it! Our house was like Bedlam[1] when we were small, but in general terms we got on well, except for the typical rows about who had nicked someone else's false eyelashes and articles of clothing that had been lent and were found at the bottom of the wardrobe rolled up in a ball. That could lead to attempted strangulation or something similar.

However, we have all kept close during the years, and now we are all getting on we look after each other as much as we can.

---

[1]. Bethlem Royal Hospital, also known as St Mary Bethlehem, Bethlehem Hospital and Bedlam, is a psychiatric hospital in London.

2
Let's Dance

Our Mum was an Angel sent from heaven. We were her seven little chicks whom she was really proud of and always found a solution to every problem. She was our rock, always there in times of woe.

When I was about 4 or 5 years old my Dad decided to send me for Ballroom dancing lessons and in a short period of time I attained my bronze, silver and gold medals from the I.D.M.A.

Soon after that, my Dad found my ideal dancing partner, and we went for classes together all over London and competed in many dancing competitions both in Ballroom and Latin American dancing. Our greatest achievement was winning the United Kingdom Juvenile Jive Championship in 1961 when I was twelve years old.

Funnily enough, one of my Dad's cousins saw the event on Pathé News in South Africa, and Dad bought the film off of them. Since then, we found out that it is on YouTube.

I never wanted to dance, but my Dad didn't give me any choice. As a kid, I didn't have a normal childhood. I was darting all over London having dancing lessons, but to tell you the truth, I am so pleased I did because dancing is my life as well as Reiki therapy.

3
Meeting M.

At the age of 20, I decided to go to Spain to work. I wanted to go abroad. I answered an add for a job as a waitress in Galicia (North West Spain), in a cafeteria, but when I arrived I was met by the agent and the job turned out to be in a sort of a nightclub. Many people called them "American Bars", meaning a sort of shifty business. However, there was absolutely nothing sordid about it, and it was nothing of the sort.

Through another waitress I met my future husband whom I shall refer to as M. He was so smarmy and good-looking that I fell for him immediately. I was only there for six weeks when he suggested I should return home because he said that the bar wasn't a suitable place for me to work.

So I took his advice and went back to London and waited every day for the postman to arrive. He sent me cassette tapes on which he spoke to me, but they were few and far between so I decided to go back because long distance was not working for us, I was crazy about him. Not long after arriving, he decided to take me to Portugal for Easter because at that time in Spain all they were showing on the television were Religious programmes.

This was Easter 1970.

4
Portugal

When we started off this trip, no one could have known what was in store for me. Our first stop was in Porto, and from there we went on to Coimbra. In a bar in Coimbra, my husband to be drew up a deal with a Portuguese guy who I will refer to as A.

The arrangement was that he would lend us a musical device to be used in the car that worked with big cartridges, which were starting to get quite popular. We were going to Lisbon and back and the agreement was to return it or buy it when we returned to Coimbra.

We enjoyed Lisbon, and on our way back we decided to make a quick stop at Nazare, a beautiful fishing village.

As we entered a Souvenir shop, at that time I had a cold sore on my lip, the owner of the store looked at me and pointed it out as he said: *"Mais a senhora vai ter uma desgraça."*

At that time I really didn't know very much Spanish or Portuguese, but it translates to "Lady, something dreadful is going to happen to you."

And he was right.

5
Sod's Law

As we approached Coimbra, M. was really putting his foot down because we were late for our meeting with A.

He asked me to hand him a cigarette, but the carton I had at the front had finished, so he reminded me that there were some more on the back seat. That was the kiss of death.

We were going over some really steep humps with not much distance between them, and he was doing about 160 km/h. Sod's law I had worn my seat belt all the way from home to Lisbon and back, but when he asked me to get one from the back seat, I took off my belt to be able to reach it.

Just at that particular moment we came over a hump and there was a traffic jam.

He slammed the brakes on, and we hit the last car who in turn hit the next one, so in all I reckon there were probably four or five cars involved. When this happened, I was thrown forward and broke the windscreen with my head. I.e. the omen of the shop owner in Nazare.

My face was bleeding heavily and I was unconscious. I only know what happened then because M. told me after.

He wrapped a T-shirt round my head. I could vaguely hear some kind of noises in the far distance, and I was taken to the Coimbra University Hospital.

6
Guardian Angel

At the hospital, I gained a little bit of consciousness and started hearing people screaming and crying in the background. The Doctor told M. that it was necessary for me to go into a Private room because I needed silence as I had a fractured skull and my face was completely cut to pieces. That wasn't just bad luck. It was meant to be.

How could that man know I was going to have an accident or something similar, and the fact that it took place when I released my seat belt? I don't know how I survived the impact, especially at that speed.

I know that I was protected by God and my Guardian Angel, and I managed to get through it. Also, another angel operated and took care of me.

Dr. Ma., I dont know right now if he is still alive, sewed my face up looking at my Passport photo.

Also at a later date I discovered that the Virgin of Fatima (I will explain further on in the book what I mean) also helped me in my recovery.

M. drove back to A Coruña and spoke to the Insurance Company, and they agreed to cover the costs of the Private room.

7
BROKEN PIECES

As well as God, good luck was on my side. When M. left, a family who had been involved in the accident with us looked after me 24/7.

There were four of them. The father, the mother, a son and a daughter. I can never thank them enough. Even Dr. Ma. brought me crushed fruit from his own home because my lips were so swollen and stitched up, and I could only eat soft food. I was so privileged to have these souls round me.

That kindness and love they showed to a complete stranger was unbelievable. I was cared for in a special, so special way, I couldn't open my eyes because they were swollen too, but one night I had such a terrible pain and a Doctor came to see me. It was about 2 in the morning, and I don't know what he used, but he got out about 8 pieces of glass that were in the back of my eye.

After 10 days they took my 108 stitches out of my face and when I saw myself in the mirror I could have died with shock. I looked like a Monster. Can you imagine all those stitches on a small face? I was no longer an attractive girl. I looked like something out of a horror film.

8
ANGELS

It was a miracle to have survived that accident.

Not long after I was released from the hospital and went back to A Coruña with M. It was very difficult to come to terms with my face cut to pieces, but M's Mum told him that he must take care of me.

After approximately six months, we went back to Coimbra to see Dr. Ma. and he couldn't believe how well my face was healing. I don't think he even recognized me. He gave me some cream to put on the scars, which was miraculous.

God bless you my beloved Dr. and my lovely Portuguese family Lança who cared for me like another member of their own family.

Even now, I think that God put them in my path at just the right time. Thank you dear God, I love you and also the intervention of the Virgin of Fatima who I deeply love too.

MIRACLES DO EXIST

And I experienced one! Thank you to all the nurses who attended me in the University Hospital of Coimbra, Portugal. They surely are angels disguised as women.

9
Eternal Beings

When I was 23 M. and I got married. All my family came over from England. It was a beautiful wedding and everyone enjoyed themselves. It was the 5th of August 1972. So long ago.

I can't really believe that my life has gone so quickly, but now, at 73, I was encouraged to write this book by my Auntie Skip (R.I.P.) to try and help humankind to understand that the life we are living is not really real and nothing is what it seems to be.

Don't be afraid dear mankind, there is nothing to be afraid of. Be brave and stand up for your rights. We have been programmed really since life began, and now it is time that we learnt that we are heavenly beings and have come here maybe as an experiment or just to learn lessons.

We are eternal beings and re-incarnate. How can I affirm this? Because I have lived many paranormal experiences, up till now not really knowing what they meant, some that left me terrified. However, I have learnt (to deal) with these experiences I have had since I was 50 years old when I meditated for the first time.

10
AND THEN CAME B.

At 26, I had my beautiful son, J.D.

He looked just like his Dad, who I truly loved. I don't think he will ever know how much.

M passed over in 2010 after suffering a great deal, but he was so brave. Never complained about anything and died with great dignity. Bless his soul.

We always had a nice home, with all the comforts so wherever you are, M, I loved you and always will.

I wrote him poems and did lots of surprises for him. He just didn't realize that I am a very sensitive person and that a red rose was just as important to me as a diamond ring.

The years passed by and in 1999, I had the pleasure of meeting B. She was my sister's friend but was the person who really taught me how to be brave.

My sister F. asked me if she could bring her to Spain on holiday. Her husband had just died of lung cancer, and she also had suffered it. Of course, I was delighted to meet her. They had worked together in Carnaby Street in the Swinging 60s.

So B. came over, and she turned out to be a wonderful person. I thoroughly enjoyed her company, and the three of us had a wonderful time together. She was a very positive sweetheart, whom we treated to a fresh cream cake every day because she couldn't get fresh cream where she lived in Canada.

11
ABOVE THE CLOUDS

She taught me a lot of things, but most of all it was absolutely magical being with her. I always think about her because she made a big change in my life. She showed me what bravery meant.

I would also like to mention my sister F. who took me to Canada to meet up with B. She knew I was frightened of flying that's why she didn't tell me we were making a stop off at Montreal.

She decided that the best thing to do for both of us was to have a drink. It was a very good idea. I thoroughly enjoyed my Vodka and Orange. I don't normally drink alcohol, but this was a special occasion. It took away most of the fear, and I was actually enjoying myself.

The Captain showed us in Newfoundland where the Titanic had sunk. How emotional was that flying over the place where it sunk. Thinking of those poor souls in those so cold waters. The orchestra carried on playing till the end. Very typical of English gentlemen in those times.

We watched a couple of English films and then landed in Montreal for a short period of time and then on to Toronto.

12
B for Bravery

At the airport, B. and her daughter were waiting for us, and she actually congratulated me for flying for such a long time. I felt ashamed of myself because she was in a wheelchair, obviously very ill, and she was consoling me instead of the other way round. B. was a very loving light soul.

She paid for my ticket from London to Toronto and then, big surprise, my dear brother-in-law paid my flight from Santiago de Compostela to London.

B.'s house was quite peculiar. Everything was decorated in black and white. The first thing she did was to tell me to go into her dressing closet and choose anything that I wanted.

Bless her, because I think she knew she didn't have much time to live. B. wherever you are, I love you. Thank you for being so kind to me.

Her daughter L. was exactly the same as her. Loving, caring, gentle and kind. We went to the highest standing telecommunication tower in Toronto that had a glass lift. I always remember that she bought our tickets to go up there, and I said "I can't go up in that lift cos I suffer from vertigo" to which she replied "If I'm in a wheelchair and dying, and I'm going up, so are you!"

To that reply, I just shut up and got on with it. I put my jacket over my head and got inside the lift, and we went up to the top of the tower. It was amazing, never seen anything like it. When we looked out of the windows, the skyscrapers looked like little buildings, I couldn't believe my eyes.

L. had to come and rescue me because when I turned round from the window I looked down at the floor, and it was made of glass!

"Oh my God!" My feet felt that they were stuck to the ground. I couldn't move. She gently encouraged me to walk forward and met me half way, that was such a relief.

Our next trip was to Niagara Falls. How amazing was that! We entered the United States at Buffalo, and quite frankly, when we reached the falls I was quite disappointed.

B. then told me that to appreciate the falls we had to go on a boat called "The Maid of the Mist." What an experience. It was just like a dream.

When we actually stopped, the boat was full thrust towards the Falls and the Captain told us that he could only remain there for thirty seconds.

I was totally gob smacked with what I saw. The hairs all over my body were standing on end. I couldn't believe I had the privilege of seeing one of the Seven Wonders of the world. The noise of the falling water was excruciating. It was a moment of time in my life that I will never forget. How honoured

I felt to be sharing this moment with this wonderful sight. Thank you to everyone who made it possible to go there.

13

THE MAPLE TREE

On my homeward flight, I suddenly realised I had lost my fear of flying. Thanks to this lovely woman whose bravery changed my life.

Imagine, I was sitting at the back of the plane on my flight from Madrid to Santiago when the flight steward was talking to an air hostess about the rear door of the plane causing problems. So I said to them: "Excuse me, if you are going to talk about the rear door, do it in the front of the plane, because if it opens during flight I'm going to be the first one to be bloody sucked out!"

When I got back to Spain, life carried on as usual, but in November 1999 my sister told me that B. had passed away.

Memories came back from the time I spent in her sitting room in Canada, looking out into the garden. It was all decked, but she had a beautiful Japanese Maple tree which really attracted my attention.

B. told me that when her mother was ill, she had travelled to England and looked after her for about six weeks. Then she went back home. She said that her and her Mum had planted the tree together and that one day, not long after her mother's death, one of the branches had risen and looked like it was waving to her.

She was sure it was her Mum saying goodbye, and I too believe it was.

Shortly after B. passed over, I was watching the television.

Actually, it was a Football match. All of a sudden, the picture went and another one appeared. It was a garden with a Japanese Maple tree. It seemed so familiar, and suddenly I recognised B.'s garden, and thought that in the same way her mother had used the tree to say goodbye to her, she was doing the same with me in the hopes that I would realise what this meant.

In a split second, I felt an intense coldness on my right side, and I knew it was her. We spoke telepathically, and she told me she wanted to thank me for everything I had done for her.

I took an article of her clothing when I was there to a Spiritual healer to see if she could help her in any way, and also wrote her a poem which was read at her funeral. She seemed over the moon that she was out of pain and was reunited with her husband.

I was so shocked I couldn't believe what was happening, but when she flew away holding her husband's hand and wearing a net dress, the football match came back on and all the lights in the flat were going off and on.

My son was on the computer at that time, and it conked out for a few minutes, so he asked me what was going on. I knew right away that there was something. It was there right in front of me. There is life after death because if there wasn't how could I have experienced what just happened.

Fear shot through my chest, I thought I had gone mad. Things like that don't happen to me, but it did. On the other hand, I was beside myself with happiness that they were together because she so wanted to be with him.

It was her deepest desire, and that desire had been accomplished.

14
Healing Scars

B. passing away made me feel very sad. It upset me, but at least I knew she was where she wanted to be.

A few weeks passed by, and I became very depressed. I was unhappy, full stop. I had no desire to do anything, and was very tired. One night, talking to my brother, I was telling him how down I felt, and he suggested that maybe meditation might help me. I asked him what to do and he explained how to go about it.

I began more or less immediately. Lit up a candle on a stool in front of me and started to scan my body from head to toe and *vice versa*, going over every part of my body and telling myself how beautiful I was.

I couldn't wait for nighttime every day. Meditating had brought peace and calm into my life, and I enjoyed every minute of it. Even gazing at a very big scar on my leg from a Melanoma (skin cancer) operation, I had when I was 38 years old became easier. It was a blow of course, but another miracle I stayed alive. I would say, "Don't worry, even though you have that great scar you are still beautiful within and without."

My plants started growing at an enormous speed. I even got myself a big photo of a human body so that when I was scanning my own I knew where all the organs were. It was amazing. I was there with myself just saying wonderful things to my body, which lifted my self-esteem so much. I think I did it so well that I actually opened a door to another dimension, and from there everything went pear shaped.

15
ENERGY

One night, when I had finished meditating, and I was just about to put out the candle, I heard like a buzzing noise coming from the corner of the left wall. When I turned round, I saw these pink and blue circles flying towards me. Later I found out that they are called "Wormholes."

They dissipated into like soot when they reached my chest and kept coming at me one after another. I was terrified. I didn't know what was going on or what I had done to make this happen. What was I going to do? Where could I hide? I just stood there like I was living a very scary Science Fiction film, really surrealistic, and they just kept coming and coming.

I was beside myself, so I ran into the bedroom and hid myself under the covers. Saying anything about it to my husband was useless, because he would have thought that I was a nutcase.

My next thought was to ring my brother, but it was too late. I was sure that he would be able to help me, so I stayed awake all night waiting to call him, and I went downstairs to a phone box (they worked in those days) to ring him at 6.00 am.

He was very surprised and said that he knew hundreds of people who meditated and had never heard anyone say that something strange had happened to them.

My brother tried to calm me down and said that he would ask some of his spiritual friends if they knew what was happening to me.

Had it been now, it would have been a different story, as I have become more and more spiritual, and perhaps I would have taken it in a different light.

I am sure I would have been shocked, but I don't think I would have been so frightened. After all, it was something wonderful, which I didn't appreciate at the time because I knew nothing about anything of this immensity.

Of course, I had to carry on meditating, trying to find out what had happened, but until this day I still don't know what this all meant.

As from that night, my life changed. I think It was an urgent wake-up call, but it felt like jumping into a swimming pool at the deep end and not knowing how to swim.

I thought I wouldn't have any more experiences, but it was only just the beginning. My body was so full of energy that my hair moved and stood on end on its own. When I was washing up, my gold bracelets just snapped off my wrist. Whenever I went out, I could see balls of energy in the sky and started to become a little psychic. Some really weird things happened to me, and I was feeling very odd.

I used to go swimming for therapy, and when getting into the shower, after coming out of the pool, I knew exactly who had been in there before me. It was like I stepped into the energy that they had left there and immediately I saw myself as that person.

Every time I closed my eyes; I got flashes of scenes, sometimes in black and white and other times in vivid colours. I didn't know what they were. I can only guess they could be of other lives I have lived. Back then, I had heard about re-incarnations, but didn't really know much about it, but now I believe in it 100%.

16
"O Rei Sol"

All this process of things that were happening to me almost drove me insane, mainly because I didn't have the slightest idea what this all meant. I couldn't find anyone to help me until a friend of mine took me to a Spiritual Centre.

There I met C., a very kind and understanding man. We meditated together and with other people who went there. He was so helpful to me that I would like to thank him for all the time he spent with me.

One night, a man entered who was from South America. I don't quite remember which country, but I think it was Peru. He told C. that he had received an important email telling him that in six or seven weeks time there was going to be an event where the Sun was going to send special energies to the Earth.

I thought, wow, that sounds fantastic. On the following Sunday, we were invited to spend that day at a friend's house in a place called Oleiros.

It was with a group of friends we had spent a lot of time with. After lunch, the men gathered to chat, usually about football, and the girls played "UNO." The card game lasted all afternoon, and we loved it.

We had some wonderful moments together, and this day was the same as many others. Or was it?

In the late afternoon, we were sitting out in the garden eating strawberries and cream just like at a posh wedding, when I turned to face the sun that was just setting and saw it started rolling like within itself, and at the same time, I saw all these globes of energy of different colours which were forming a circle round it. It was just like a firework display.

I looked at everyone else and asked the woman next to me if she could see anything funny in the sky, and she said she couldn't see anything unusual. It was if that firework display was only for my eyes. I then realised that this was the event that the South American gentleman had referred to, and I was witnessing it six or seven weeks before it was really supposed to take place. I think this was what they call "The Sun dance."

Once again, I was really scared. Was I going mad or what? I wondered why it had happened in Oleiros, and as I loved doing anagrams on words I put the word Oleiros in front of me and started juggling the letters until I arrived at "O Rei Sol" which, in Gallego[2] means "The Sun God."

Also, if you look at the word Galicia, it has "Gaia" in it, another name for Mother Earth. Beautiful Mother Earth, bless her.

The next day I told C. what had happened to me, and he took it very seriously. Every night I said the Lord's Prayer and asked Archangel St. Michael to protect me. I made my husband take down all the mirrors in my house because I felt I was being watched.

At night, it was impossible to sleep because of the visions, the ghosts and the fear I had. I really don't know how I got through all of that, and it still continues today. I was driving myself insane. Not sleeping day or night and wondering what was going to happen to me next.

---

2. The region where I live is Galicia, and its local language, besides Spanish, is Gallego.

17

Being Safe

All I did was cry... I could hardly eat anything, and in a matter of about two months I lost 10 kilos. Obviously, I couldn't carry on like this, I needed to have medication to survive and let me sleep for a few hours.

So reluctantly I went to a psychiatrist. He asked me to explain what my problem was, and he said that even though I was talking sense, these kind of things mainly don't happen its all in your mind, and scientifically they can't be proved.

Once I got all my medication, it was a blessing. At least I could sleep during the night, which is, of course, the worst thing. I just cried and cried because what was hurting me wasn't my body, it was my soul. I asked M. to take me to see a Priest because maybe I was possessed. The one we visited more or less said "Pull yourself together, life is wonderful and here, take this book I have written and read it."

Furthermore, I asked him to give me an exorcism, and eventually he agreed. He said some prayers with a cross in his hand and when he flicked the holy water on me, I felt a pain shoot right through my body, so there must have been something there. I was an easy target, because I was so low and depressed.

The days passed on, and the weeks too. The only thing that I wanted to do was to stay in bed and sleep, to try and forget everything. When I was asleep, I felt safe and my contact with the outside world had finished. I was frightened to go out and only wanted to be where I felt safe.

Can you imagine a situation where you don't know exactly what is happening to you? You want to run away, but there is nowhere to run to. You want to hide, but there is nowhere to hide, either. I would force myself to go for a little walk along the promenade. Maybe sit on a bench and stare at a tree. If I closed my eyes, I was someone else, maybe from another era. I would see people walking with horses and carts instead of doggies, just crazy stuff.

One night, one of my Reiki colleagues phoned me late and said that she had burned herself in the shower. She said that suddenly the water came out boiling hot and scalded her. She asked me to imagine the scene and see if I could discover what had happened.

As I imagined the scene, I saw an old man banging on the floor with his walking stick, saying that this was his house and he didn't want anyone there. For that reason, I suppose he was able to manipulate the water and wanted to harm her so that she would leave.

Obviously, it was a former owner or tenant of the flat. I told him that he was no longer the owner of this apartment, and he shouldn't take his anger out on my friend. After that, I imagined putting cream on her burnt face and telling her not to worry because everything was going to be OK. The next morning, she phoned me and told me that the burn marks had gone, and she was fine. After that she cleaned and blessed the house, and she never noticed anything strange again. He must have left, I hope he went to the light.

I also had another incident with her. We were at class at our healing centre and were talking about allergies. My teacher taught me to create archetypes to try and find out why people were allergic to different things.

She mentioned that she was allergic to cow's milk. On that same note, I decided to do an archetype and saw a lady milking a cow. A little girl came close to where her Mum was, and the cow kicked the bucket and frightened the life out of her. It was very traumatic for her, and the fear that she experienced turned out to be her allergy to cow's milk.

The human mind is so mysterious. She told me that it was exactly what happened to her. Amazing, don't you think?

When I started having experiences when I first meditated, at night I would close my eyes and see myself in outer space. I could jump or fly from one planet to another. I thought to myself Blimey NASA has to spend a bomb to send rockets or whatever to outer space and I can get there just by closing my eyes.

On one occasion I saw myself sitting apparently in the centre of the solar system. I knew I was sitting on something, but at the beginning I couldn't understand what it was until I heard a noise like water being spouted out.

Then I realised it was coinciding with the breathing of a huge animal and I saw it. It was a gigantic tortoise that was breathing and spouting out the water and I was sitting on its shell.

I don't have these kind of visions now, but the times that I visited outer space were numerous. Shame I don't get them anymore, they were so exciting, but I suppose it all had to take its course in the way that it was supposed to.

God, I realise now how powerful my mind was. To be able to travel to outer space in a second was unthinkable but lucky for me it happened and those images will remain in my mind forever. I was blessed but didn't realise it at that time.

18
The Universe Speaking

As a Reiki group, we often went to the beach every month and offered a meditation to the full moon. One night, there were about six of us, and we went to a sort of Pagoda not far from the beach. We started our beautiful meditation to honour the moon and all of a sudden we heard the sea roar really loudly during about 10 seconds.

We all looked at each other, and we all had the same thought that the sea was thanking us for carrying out the meditation because of our love for Mother Earth and the Universe. It was a unique experience, just like how was it possible that the sea was giving us six women such a tribute.

The same sort of thing happened when I was doing my third course of Reiki. We were at our masters' house and we went outside to perform a Meditation called "Meditación del corazón", the heart meditation. It's a type of dance, very beautiful, all in sequence together with the corresponding music. During that dance, on a very hot day, a breeze blew past us only for a few minutes and then stopped.

Once again, we shared the same feeling that it was the Universe thanking us. A similar sensation to the one we had on the beach. How can you believe that the Universe is really talking to you? It's really incredible. How honoured I have been to be able to experience these episodes of love shown to my companions and me. Hard to believe, but we all knew deep down in our souls that it was happening, we shivered and got goose pimples, this was REAL.

Another time, some of my Reiki companions and I decided that we wanted to plant an Oak tree. So the ladies who organized it, S. and M., bought the tree and it was decided, that we would plant it in the Pazo of Faramello, which is about 10 km from Santiago de Compostela. *Pazo* in English means Manor House.

My friends S. and M. knew the owner of the Manor House, and he allowed us to plant the tree there. When we arrived there was a storm and it was raining cats and dogs. We were very upset because the idea of planting the tree seemed impossible. This gentleman invited us inside for some cheese and wine. So we all went inside escaping from the downpour.

We were in there for about twenty minutes and when we opened the door we were stunned. The rain had subsided and the sun was shining full blast. Immediately we went outside and this very kind man showed us all round this beautiful Manor House. There was even a chapel inside.

We took about an hour to go round the manor and then decided to plant the tree. I swear that when he put the last shovel of earth on it; it started to rain again and the storm came back. I think that this was another example of the Universe, helping us to achieve our goal.

Completely and utterly uncanny, but by now with the two earlier experiences with the sea and the breeze we had experienced yet another sign that we and the Universe are one. How beautiful is that.

I have had the privilege of witnessing many beautiful things. The ones that I have told you about are the most important ones, the ones that stick out most in my mind.

I never ever thought in my lifetime that anything like this would happen to me, not in my wildest dreams. The only thing I really know is that I feel so honoured to have seen these wonderful things. I even used to feel the earth moving under my feet, and I knew there was going to be an earthquake. Sure enough the following day or the day after I would hear on the news that there had been an earthquake somewhere in the world.

God has shown me his unconditional love many times, and perhaps enticed me to tell you all that it is time. We must "WAKE UP" and not be bullied by others to take away our freedom. Fight for it because we are the 99% and the elite only 1%.

That means we have a great chance of survival if we all stick together so that their plans to eliminate the majority of the world population never come about!

God save mankind!!!

19

UNDER THE SPOTLIGHT

One friend of mine, a great natural medicine doctor, was using a special programme for Holistic Healing. In this practice she would test you with some discs called "Chakrons", and whatever state of mind you were in, she would find out through it. The result was a colour and the corresponding music.

On various occasions, my need of a colour was red. I had to lie down in a bed covered with like nylon nets, all rigorous white, and she would put a strong red spotlight along with the music.

The different types of music, that you heard with large earphones, were loud and impressive. Every time I was under the red light, and it's music, I saw the same scenes over and over again. Always in very vivid colours, I saw two women putting a baby in a basket into a river. They were dressed as in very old times. My gut feeling, and I think I'm right, was that these women were Moses's mother and sister, and of course that the baby in the basket was Moses. That scene was so vivid that I couldn't work out where I came into this equation.

Was it me putting the baby in the Nile? Was it me who was in the basket? Was I Moses's mother or his sister?

It's funny that since I was a kid I was obsessed with the 10 Commandments and even today they always stick in my mind and are sacred to me.

After this scene, there was very beautiful music, a Viennese Waltz. I saw myself dancing in a great big ballroom with a beautiful dress, but when I turned round I saw my partner was Donald Duck. I think that my subconscious was not allowing me to see who I was dancing with, but whenever I had therapy, the unknown person was always disguised as Donald Duck.

I don't ever watch cartoons. I don't like them for some reason unknown to me. They disturb me terribly. Maybe something happened to me once when I was watching them and associate this, but who knows. I certainly don't.

I always say that, even though I've had lots of experiences, the only thing I know is that I know nothing.

20

THE KEY

My friend took me to see a South American psychologist. After having a chat with him, he put on a relaxation tape with an English speaking man with a terrible Spanish accent.

However, the therapy was very effective, and right at the end he said, "remember a decade you would like to return to." So I thought, I'd love to go back to the sixties. I was expecting to see the Beatles or the Rolling Stones, but instead, I saw a cave man dragging a rope sack full of big stones.

I couldn't work that one out. When I questioned him about what I had seen, he said "that's normal, you asked to go back to the sixties, but you should have said 1960s." Amazing, don't you think? I had returned to the decade of 60 BC.

After a while, I decided to have a go at Yoga. I couldn't do all the postures, but mainly I did stretching, and it helped my back a little. I spoke to the teacher about the things that were happening to me, and he suggested that I might like Reiki, so he gave me the phone number of the Director of a centre where I could do the necessary courses.

I phoned her, and she encouraged me to try. She told me that there was a course in Santiago de Compostela for the first degree. So I put my name down and have never looked back.

I really enjoyed the course, and I mean really, really loved it. It brought a new meaning to my life, to be able to be of help to others, and also, the other members of my group are so lovely. We love each other more than words can say, and they were very open about most things, so I was very comfortable talking to them about all the things that I had experienced. It's clear to me, that only with love and affection you can be nourished.

My Reiki Master, whom I will refer to as J. was incredible making the day very light-hearted, and we were all full of love by the time the day was over.

Here you are always just a humble channel using Universal Energy and your hands. To have a session of Reiki is like being in another world.

Nothing strange, just receiving energy in your seven energy points (Chakras). You feel so warm, so loved, so relaxed you don't want it to end. A great remedy for stress. It is just as wonderful to receive it as giving it. You can feel the love that the other person is giving to you. Sometimes it's like being in Mummy's arms again, when you were a baby.

I did three courses, but only to the stage of being able to give therapy, but not to initiate anyone. That's the way I wanted it to be. At that stage of my life, I didn't want to complicate anything, just enjoy these meetings of meditation, dancing, and feeling an immense love I had never felt before.

21

HELPING OTHERS

One day, the Director of my centre suggested I went to see a Reiki Master near Vigo. She said he was a very good therapist. So I went to see him, and he told me that I was going to be an important key in the changing of mankind.

I looked at him in dismay. What was he talking about? I was only a girl from South London with a Church of England Mum and a Jewish dad. I told him he was mistaken but couldn't help thinking, "what did he mean?"

I didn't tell anyone at the time, but he asked me to go back the following week so that another Reiki Master, apparently his teacher, could see me. So the next week, I went again and met his teacher. She also agreed about the matter. This left me bewildered.

After that, on leaving, I saw some trees in the distance. My only desire was to share this with them. So off I went and sat down under a tree, and started to cry. I cried for a long time, because apart from being stunned by what he had said, I felt really honoured that possibly I could be a key to the future of mankind. I didn't know in what way, but I just couldn't get it through my head that maybe there was truth in it.

I have been waiting ever since then for something really important to happen, but it never did. However, I now think that I know what my task was. I had to write this book to disclose the things that have happened to me and try in some way to take away from millions of people the thought of being scared to die.

To be able to do that would be a wonderful achievement for me. God only knows I wanted to help other people in whatever way I could and this maybe an opportunity, through my words, to do so.

Even though I consider I have had both, terrible experiences and good ones too, I am not really scared of anything. I don't really care what other people think about me, because I know who I am, and for me that is sufficient.

22

The Book

I had to write this book because I always wanted to, and it was only through my darling Auntie Skip's encouragement that I am doing it.

My Auntie Skip, God bless her soul, passed over in 2019. Since our Mum passed, she had been the family's rock, but I think she felt it was time to be with her husband, uncle Michael. They adored each other and she was longing to be with him again. She had been ill for a long time. She couldn't walk, and was confined to an armchair in the lounge 24/7. As she couldn't go upstairs due to her mobility issues and she found it was much easier to do so.

She loved talking with Mummy about all the strange and funny things that happened to them during the war. She was a cheeky gal and so was my Mum.

Since I meditated in 1999 I became a little psychic but nothing really I could put my finger on. But in the last few months, 2022, I kept getting glimpses of her, and she didn't look very happy. These glimpses only lasted a matter of seconds, and made me very worried. I felt like she was trying to tell me something, or maybe, that she might be "trapped."

I really don't know, but the case was I felt I needed to find out and try and get in contact with her to see if she needed my help in any way, for my own peace of mind.

My brother led me to a good medium and made an appointment for me. As he actually lives in England, we obviously had to have a video conference to speak to each other. This virtual encounter was one of the happiest moments of my life.

When I spoke to him, he had already been in contact with my Auntie. He referred to her as this "wonderful lady", and she told him straight off that I had got the wrong end of the stick. In fact, she said that she was doing very well on the other side, she had no more pain, she was with my dear Uncle and when she passed over the whole family were waiting for her.

My Auntie said that they congratulated her for being able to live on Earth for 94 years. It was a very great achievement, as maybe Earth is the most difficult planet to live on, probably because we have emotions and everyone sooner or later suffers through love or loss of relatives... It's not easy.

Apart from that, we must take into consideration, that we don't come with an "instruction book" under our arm. We have to learn through our mistakes, and unfortunately, some people repeat the same thing over and over again.

She also said that she had been trying to contact me because she was worried about me. She knew I had numerous health issues, but she wanted to help me because I was a strong woman like her (bless), and she didn't like to see me suffering. She mentioned she had been stroking my tummy, aware of my problems in that area, and also my terrible back pain, which she also knew about.

I try to carry on regardless, and go out dancing at the weekends, meet up with my English friends twice a week, and go out as much as I can. When I go dancing, and I'm in a lot of pain, I don't let it stop me. I just take an extra pain killer and I'm off.

23

BLACKCURRANT CHEESECAKE

During the conversation with the Canadian medium, he mentioned that my aunt was showing him a piece of blackcurrant cheesecake, and while eating it, she explained, "life is like this. The slower you eat it, the more wonderful it tastes. But if you stuff it into your mouth, and gulp it down, it just goes, and you don't get the same sense of flavouring it."

Other matters, came up in the meeting, she told him to put me at ease about my economic worries, and if I would have enough money to last me until I pass over (I guess we all worry about money if we haven't got it). She also suggested that I looked into natural medicine to help me with my health problems and added that when I went out dancing, I should dress up nicely, do my makeup and try to look really sexy. That made me laugh! I always tried my best to look nice, and why not say it, sexy too!

Then, she encouraged me to write a book about all the things I knew about. I have always wanted to write a book about my paranormal experiences, but never told her about it.

Then the medium told me that I was quite charismatic and had a very vibrant aura. He also said that people would listen to me and believe what I say.

This made all the difference, and the fact that she told me to do it, encouraged me so much, I was thrilled to bits. Obviously, now was the right time to start writing this book, maybe not before. Everything in life occurs at the right time.

I thanked the medium, and also my brother, for bringing this man into my life. More than anything else, I could rest at ease knowing that Auntie Skip was safe and happy, out of pain and with her beloved husband and family.

This lovely gentleman helped me out so much. Thank God I met him! I was so stressed out about my aunt. He told me that our loved ones, although on a different frequency, are always with us, caring for us and guiding us.

When we say that we don't believe in life after death because nobody comes back to tell you, I think its because that person only lives one life as that person. When they pass on, they re-incarnate as someone else, so we can only reach them in the spirit world.

I am saying this, but please don't take it as being the correct truth, it's just something that came to me right at the moment I am writing now. I respect everyone's opinion, and you all have the right to have your own ideas about these different subjects. It's not a case of trying to persuade someone that you are in the right, it's about listening to and respecting other people's point of view with the respect that you desire for yourself.

When I decided to write this book, I began by handwriting it because I love doing so, and then passed it on to the computer. I don't have much knowledge about this device, but I have managed to do it, with effort and patience.

So, now you know the reason I am writing this book. Doesn't matter if it is successful or not? Not really. The most important thing was to do it, and hope I have done something worthwhile.

24

Come Together

Deep down, I hope that my Auntie, together with my Mum and Dad, so loved who are with her, will be proud of me. And I wish for the readers to like it too. I really would be so pleased if this book brought comfort to you in some way, to know that life carries on after death, and to have hope for the future for your families, especially your children that hopefully things will get better.

I send you all so much love from the bottom of my heart. I know you are suffering so much, so am I, but maybe with all our hearts together we can create enough love to rid us of all the horrible things that we have lived over the past couple of years.

Come on!!! Let's all do it together, and try and make the world a better place to live in. Together we can do it!! Kill your enemies with love. That's what my darling Mum always used to say. I didn't encounter anyone wiser than her ever, and I miss her so much.

Finding out, after that reading, that my spiritual family are with me too, is a great comfort when I sometimes feel lonely. It taught me not to worry so much about dying, because all my loved ones are still there in their spiritual form, but just on another plane.

We are all one. It's strange how nearly all of us are frightened of dying, but really we don't die, only our body does. Our spirit is everlasting, and I am convinced we have had previous lives too.

I often ask God to forgive me if I hurt or killed anyone in another life, but I think it is so logical that we have. If not how on earth would we know the difference between Good and Bad? These themes have troubled me all my life, but at the same time intrigue me.

At last, the pieces of the puzzle are fitting and I am finding answers to some of my questions. They come at the right time. Therefore, with all these reasonings, I don't like to judge anyone because we could all have been murderers or whatever in our previous lives and not even know.

I have always wondered about Nefretiti. In some of the images we have seen of her, one of her eyes has no iris[3]. I never found out the reason, so if any of the readers has a clue, please let me know.

---

3. When the iconic bust of Nefertiti, part of the Egyptian Museum of Berlin collection, was first discovered, there was no quartz to represent the iris of the left eyeball. It was then assumed that the quartz iris had fallen out, but the missing eye also led to speculation that she may have suffered from an ophthalmic infection and lost her left eye. The presence of an iris in other statues of her seem to contradict this possibility, but we will may never know.

25

BELIEVE IN MIRACLES

At the beginning of the book, I told you that the Virgin of Fatima had looked after me at the accident. The time has come to explain how I found that out.

After my second course of Reiki, I had to do a meditation during 21 days. It consisted in dividing your age between 21, and meditate each day about your life at that day and age. When I got to the time when my age of 20 was included, I saw myself at the hospital in Coimbra, in bed, I was surrounded by angels.

My God, I started to cry. Who was I to get this protection? Immediately, I knew that the Virgin of Fatima had sent them to look over me. It was so emotional, really, seemed impossible, but they were there for sure. I spoke to a friend, who was also a medium, and she told me that the Virgin Fatima knew I wanted to go and thank her for what she had done for me. But she also said that it was too cold and too long a journey for me, and to wait for another time, and that she completely understood why I shouldn't go.

I finally went to Fatima two years ago, and at long last, I was able to thank her, for all she had done to save my life. She is known to be miraculous, and certainly she was with me. I'm so grateful to her because if it wasn't for her, I wouldn't be sitting down writing this book now.

I imagine you find it almost impossible to believe some of the things I have told you. Sometimes, I really can't believe them myself. But I can assure you they did happen.

26
BEAUTIFUL EARTH

Nowadays, I feel closer to God than I ever have, and to the Holy family. I know I have been protected all these years because I have escaped death quite a few times.

Some nights I have a chat with God, I tell him things just like he was my brother. I complain about this, that and the other, but I feel assured he is near me. He is my father and Mary my mother. They make me feel so loved. It's a different type of love, a Spiritual one, that through meditation I was able to find after a long struggle.

There are times, when I am tidying up, washing up or even cooking, which I don't like, I have to leave everything, sit down and meditate, just to let go of the things I am thinking about, because quite honestly, I think that our mind is our worst enemy.

I would love people to think that lots of tragedies that occur have nothing to do with God (that is only my opinion). Us humans, in general, are selfish, greedy and jealous and have many dark thoughts (I include myself). Things have always been like that since the beginning of time.

We are also slaughtered by rules and regulations since we are born. It's always "Don't do this" or "Don't do that." It seems to me like we have been programmed to obey by an unknown source, although more or less I know where this is all coming from. But my belief is "What goes round, comes round" you can't escape. Sooner or later you will receive your own medicine.

Why can't we change!!! Why can't we be different? Why can't we change all this palaver and learn to say no to certain things that are completely unfair. Make the Earth a wonderful place to live in, where everybody is equal. No famines, no wars, no poorness or illness, only love and harmony.

Sometimes I wonder how God is so patient with us and is always giving us a new chance, and it always ends up the same. The Earth is a beautiful place to live in; the only thing that spoils it, are human beings.

I know there are a lot of good people out there, but lately everything is doom and gloom. You can't even watch the news anymore it's all so depressing...

Anyway let's change the subject.

27
Let's Wake Up

Ever since I was a child, I have always felt lost. I don't seem to fit in anywhere. I've never felt excited about getting back home, because I don't think that anywhere I have lived seemed like home. The nearest to that was when I used to spend a couple of months with Mummy every summer.

I went back to England many times, but when my Dad died, I stayed longer. I never wanted to come back, but I didn't want to stay there, either. I have lived in Spain nearly all my life, and I have my son, my grandson and all my friends here, but most of the time I feel lonely.

There is no-one to say good morning or goodnight to. I have quite rightly been picked up on this by my family, but you get so used to not saying it when you live on your own. I have been a widow for 12 years now, but have never found up till now anyone to share my life with. Apart from that, I think it would be difficult to live with someone else after all this time because as you get older you get a lot of hang-ups. Anyway, my heart is still open to love.

So I have had a lot of therapies, mainly to try and find out where I belong, and also to try and find peace of mind. But at the end of the day, I really don't know much more than I did at the beginning. Maybe for some unknown reason to me, I didn't want to re-incarnate.

Everyone has their own journey, and even if you seek help from others, when it comes to making decisions you are the only one who can do it. It's not worth worrying about things that might never happen. It's a waste of energy. I say that and should practice what I preach.

It's time now for mankind to "wake up" and realise that what we are living right now is a shock to our systems. I bet you never thought you would have to suffer a Pandemic in your lifetime for over two years in this day and age?

I feel like we have chosen to be here right now to witness the biggest change in world history. In my humble opinion, we will ascend to the 5th Dimension, and hopefully our lives will change drastically for the better. However, time will tell. It has been so difficult for us, and we have been very obedient, except for some brave people out there.

I think that all this manipulation of the human species by the dark side (Satanic followers) is coming to an end. What I have written may be censured, but no worries, I'm not scared. We are controlled by fear. That is why we always obey. For some people, it has been absolute panic, and I can understand that completely. We weren't even allowed to say goodbye to our loved ones when they passed over. It's all so sad, isn't it?

I am trying to give you a glimpse of hope for the future. God and the Universe are perfectly aware of what is going on, and they are trying to stop it from happening. They will succeed, as the light will prevail in the end. So I beg you not to worry too much, because this has all been planned years ago, and it will all fall into place at the right time.

I have always thought that aliens will come down to help us, not to attack us. I'm sure there are wars in the Universe too. Once I had a vision of angels fighting against demons. This is a constant challenge between good and bad. I don't want you to fear dying because you have died many times before, and you don't even know it.

28

REGRESSIONS

As I told you before, I have been in and out of therapies since all these strange things happened to me. On one occasion, a friend recommended a very good therapist to me. What I didn't realise at the time was that she was a therapist of regressions (healing of previous lives).

I liked her very much, and the first couple of times I went to see her I was comfortable, and that is important for me. However, the first time I did a regression, I wasn't sure if I liked it or not. It was amazing how she got into my subconscious. I saw myself as a Pharaoh being embalmed. I could see all the bright colours of the place where a man was covering me with oils, and of course, I presumed I was dead and being prepared for my eternal rest.

These were like flashes of scenes, really hard to describe When she asked me what I had died of, I said that I had had a heart attack. I saw myself as a young man, and somehow I knew I had a wife and a son.

She insisted that I related to her why I had had a heart attack, and I just suddenly said "I was poisoned", without even thinking about it.

She told me to face my enemies, which I did and tell them to give me back the energy that they had stolen from me by taking my life, which they did, and I in return I had to give back the energy of all the innocent slaves that had died with me in my burial chamber. I then had to imagine opening up a crack in the wall, as a route of escape for them, and I saw them shoot out of it very quickly before I closed it. After that, she started to move the poison through my body with her hands, and I swear I was heaving, nearly vomiting.

After we finished the session, I couldn't believe that it was me telling this story. It was so real. I said to her that I must have made it all up, but she disagreed. Then I thought to myself, how is it possible to tell her this story with such detail?

At school, I got my highest mark ever, 77 out of 100, for history. It was an exercise I did about the Pyramids. Like a lot of other people, as a young girl of 10, I was fascinated by everything to do with Egypt. Maybe that fascination was because I had actually lived there in another life.

You see, when I say nothing is what it seems, I mean how could I have told her that if was in another body? How could I remember that, and via my subconscious they came to life? It's like you can't believe what you just narrated. Why didn't I remember that anyway, without going into my subconscious?

All this was doing my head in. I've found out so many things since my awakening, because I think we are living in a Universe where two and two don't make four.

I have read that people who receive transplants of different organs, often take up hobbies that their donor did, like painting and other things. It's as if as well as receiving an organ from another body, that organ kind of changes its new owner's habits or hobbies.

29
MONSTERS

The next time I went to see the therapist of regressions, once into my subconscious, I saw a baby in my womb that was half human, half monster.

Oh my God! What next!

Then, I saw myself inside a spaceship surrounded by grays. When I went on board, I greeted the pilots of the ship. They all knew me, and I knew them. There were glass tubes everywhere, with hybrids inside, but it all seemed very familiar.

My obvious thought was that I had been abducted many times, probably from my bed, but I don't know how I got to the spaceship or how I returned.

On this occasion, I saw myself as a young girl in this life, maybe eleven or twelve years old. I'm not quite sure, but the next thing I saw was that I was strapped to a very narrow bed made of some type of metal. The bed started to move forward, and I saw a Cyclops in front of me. I'm sure they forced him to have intercourse with me because he looked really scared, like he was doing something he didn't want to do. How can I describe him?... He looked like Chewbacca from Star Wars, but only had one eye in the middle of his forehead.

At one time, during this regression, I could only see darkness. I was getting really tired. The therapist explained that when there is something that you don't want to see, probably that is very hurtful to you, then blackness sets in.

She told me that there was a light on my right-hand side, obviously imaginary, and asked me to switch it on. When I did so, I saw right in front of me in vivid colours the Cyclops, and I screamed out "It's that f------ monster again."

How on earth could this happen?

The image was so clear and vivid it seems impossible to believe. That was enough for me, and I decided not to do any more regressions. My life was complicated enough without adding previous lives to complicate it even more.

I was furious to find out that I had been abducted. How dare they do that without my permission? Now, that anger has subsided a bit because I read that these beings are in the 4th dimension, and they carry out their experiments on humans that are in the 3rd dimension. In the same way that humans carry out experiments with animals, who supposedly are in the 2nd dimension.

I had another scene where I was lying on the metal bed, and I heard them talking. They were saying, "well we've done most things to her. What shall we do now?" Then I heard another voice from a different part of the place, who said "That's enough!"

Anyway, it happened, and there was nothing I could do about it because it's the past and you can't change it.

30

Lights in the Sea

One afternoon, I was in bed with a slight touch of flu. My dog Sally was sitting on the bed too. I started hearing a buzzing noise and Sally must have heard it too.

Well, this was really too much.

Suddenly, I saw three little spaceships come through a closed window. They were the shape of fried eggs, and from what I could see, they didn't have any crew.

Both of us just sat there in astonishment.

I would say that maybe they were scouts for a Mother ship and were investigating, I don't know what. We have to take into consideration, that they came down a patio. The building, if I remember rightly, had six floors and an attic flat. The same way they came through the window, they went out the door.

Anyone would think that they were crazy seeing that, let's be fair.

Then, to top it all up, a friend of mine phoned me the following morning to tell me that they had interviewed her son on the radio because he saw three lights in the sea at a place called Mera. I realised at once that she was talking about the ships that had visited me the day before.

I didn't say a word, but confirmed in my mind that it really had happened and definitely wasn't my imagination.

31

DANCING TO LIFE

When meditating, it seems to me that I opened up a door to another dimension, and although I can't say this, that or the other, it surely has changed my life.

I knew, as a channel, I had some healing abilities, but I could help some people and not others. Not in a therapy, but usually when I was dancing, because then my vibes are so high.

I'm in a different world, where the music transports me away to a dreamland, and when it's time to go home, I always said to myself "back to the shitty reality." I really feel that for people who are suffering depression, it is one of the greatest therapies ever.

There was a time I offered to give free dancing classes to the doctors and nurses in the local hospital. I spoke to a woman who was in charge of Social Services, and she was quite rude to me, like was I joking, as the doctors didn't have any free time for anything, let alone dancing classes.

Even when my friend and I went round to the Institutions offering free Reiki, we were turned down. No one was interested, so we lost heart. It is known, that for terminal patients it is very helpful and also helps them with the passing over.

We were both so enthusiastic to help, but we came to the conclusion that our help was rejected, and why try and convince people who are not interested. It's all about protocol, and they are not willing to try anything outside what their rules and regulations allow them.

How sad it is when you have something so special to offer, gladly and sincerely, offered with the conviction that you can help people who are distressed and suffering, and no one is interested.

Dancing for Doctors and nurses would be a wonderful thing. It takes stress away, makes you laugh when you make mistakes… It was about just showing the basic steps of most of the dances, enough to defend yourself at any dance hall. I wasn't going to train them to go on *Strictly Come Dancing*[4], but those who have watched these programmes know the great happiness that it brings to the competitors. Someone who thought they could never dance, and said they had two left feet, were trained by professionals and achieved fantastic results.

Life is about being happy and enjoying ourselves. Laughing and having a good time, whatever hobby we enjoy. I'm pretty sure that God would love us to enjoy our lives instead of being bad-tempered, miserable and depressed. Although I have many health issues, I won't let them stop me from doing anything I want to do.

I usually go dancing at the weekend (sometimes till the early hours of the morning). If I am in a lot of pain, I just take an extra painkiller and get on with it. If I'm not too bad, I can dance the night away.

Obviously, I have to stop between dances to have a rest, so that I can get my breath back. Other times, when I can't, I like to sit and watch other people enjoying themselves. It gives me great pleasure to watch other people dancing.

---

4. British television dance contest in which celebrities partner with professional dancers to compete.

A lot of times, when I dance with people, when I touch their shoulders or hands normally, everything starts to crack, especially their fingers. I can feel it, but they can't, or I sense rumbling sensations in their bodies, but I don't know what it means.

Lots of times, when people touch me, their stomach starts to rumble. I don't know the reason for this either. It's even hard for me to hold a mobile phone, because I get funny sensations up my arms from the radio activity, and it makes my muscles jump.

By the way, I'm just like any other human being. I get ill, and have problems, like everyone else. There must be other people who have different sensations like me, but somehow, one has to learn to accept it.

32
STONEHENGE

I would like you to know, too, that I am blessed with a beautiful family. My nephew and his wife invited me to have a holiday on the Isle of Wight, for a week, in 2019. My sister, my nephew's Mum, came along too. We had a great time stuffing scones and tea everywhere, and visited quite a few places, but one in particular became very special to me, Osborne House in East Cowes, the summer residence of Queen Victoria and Prince Albert.

The house was beautiful, I love going round these places, touching the walls to see if any images go through my mind and was in awe of the lovely paintings and sculptures there.

It seemed that they were very much in love, for the amount of presents they bought each other. I hope that is true. It's a wonderful thing to be in love and have a special bond with your loved one.

How gorgeous that must be.

When I came outside, I walked towards a low wall and closed my eyes. Most of the paranormal things I see (not always), are when I have my eyes closed. Low and behold, I saw an Army marching up the hill with their rifles on their shoulders. The image was bright and colourful. They were soldiers who were wearing red jackets and dark blue trousers. They weren't fighting right then.

I opened my eyes and they were gone.

After asking my nephew if there had been any wars on this island, he wasn't really able to answer me at that moment.

When I got home, I started to look up battles, etc. on the Isle of Wight, and found that in 1545, the French had tried to invade the island. I think that in those days their uniforms were either blue or red, all according to the desire of the General who was in charge.

My God, I realised that just in a blink I had gone back 500 years in time. I cannot validate this information I have given, because 1545 is the last known attempt of the French trying to invade the island, so it could have been before that. I am just telling you what I saw and the information I managed to rustle up on the net.

When we left the Isle of Wight, we went back to my nephew's house, which wasn't all that far from Stonehenge.

I didn't have to persuade him too much to take me because I think he was quite interested himself. I had dreamt about going to Stonehenge for years. It's one of the Earth's Chakras.

When we started out, it wasn't a very warm day. There were my nephew, his two sons and my sis. When we got there, the weather was miserable, but there were sunny spells from time to time.

My sister said that she didn't want t to go, and that she was going to stay in the cafeteria. So off we went on the bus, from the main entrance to where the stones were.

I was very excited and wondering what impression I was going to get from the site. As we were arriving, the sun was shining, and my nephew and the kids only had T-shirts on. I was amazed at the colour of the grass. I don't think I have ever seen grass so green.

Through the window of the bus, my first impression was that it was a graveyard and was longing to get off the bus to get closer and close my eyes to see what I could get. However, just as we came down the steps of the bus, the sky suddenly turned black, and there was a great downpour of rain. We couldn't possibly go to the stones. We got soaked to the skin in a few seconds, so we had to get back up again on the bus.

That was a real freak episode of weather, and when we got back to the main entrance, the sun was shining like nothing had happened. He was very surprised and said that that was something he wouldn't forget in a hurry. My nephew promised me that when I went back, he would take me again, because he too was stunned by what happened.

33
Among Trees

At this point, I would like to mention my brother S. He helped me so much in every way. When I was going through this trauma or miracle, I really don't know what to call it. I stayed with him for some weeks, for which I will always be grateful.

S. put me in contact with nature, something I had never really thought about. He made me take a walk twice a day, in the morning and in the afternoon, right through a lot of greenery. At that stage I began to cuddle trees, and now they have become my great love and my best friends.

Through the window, coming down the stairs in his house, I could see the enormous oak tree in the garden. When I looked at it, it had a beautiful mauve aura all round it.

Truly, the area where he was living then was magical. He made me plant different plants in the front garden so that I would have close contact with the Earth. This therapy was so good for me, it made me someone new. I had missed out on all this because I'd always lived in towns and had never appreciated the beauty of nature.

Thank God for the trees. I spoke to them, and they listened to me. I always asked permission to touch them first, and sometimes they answer me.

In 2019, I was walking along the promenade near my home. It was November, I think, and I went up to one of the trees. I told it that I loved it and asked if it had anything to tell me. It then said, "Beware the Ides of March." It didn't register, but now I realise it was warning me about the Pandemic, which started in March 2020 (on the 14th, Spain declared the state of emergency).

The Ides of March were a warning to watch out for betrayal or misfortune. The term refers to March 15th, the day on which Roman Emperor Julius Caesar was assassinated in 44 B.C. For this reason, it has become associated with bad omens, betrayal and misfortune. How appropriate.

On many other occasions I got messages from my dearest trees. Once, when I was in Vigo, a tree told me to "stay away from blue." Did it mean the blue beam? I'm not sure.

One other time, a tree near my home kept repeating to me "ammonia." Why was it saying that? Then it came to me. I was told to put a glass of water with ammonia on my bedside table to keep spirits from bothering me, but that morning I had changed it for water with rock salt in it, for no reason. It was telling me to put the ammonia back, probably because it was more effective.

I used to go out with my music and dance with the trees, something I really loved doing. I talked to them, cried with happiness to be with them and just loved them for all the wonderful things that they do for us. I even wrote a poem about trees, because I need them to survive. They are so important to mankind.

When I am tired, I ask them to give me enough energy to walk to the next one to ask the same thing. They always rise to the occasion, and if I don't get to cuddle them for a couple of days, I get miserable. I feel that they need me too, my love, which comes from deep inside. People always stare at me. Some laugh, some smile, some must think I'm mad, but I bet they would love to have the feeling I have when I embrace them. "Los quiero con locura."

34

MESSAGES

At Easter this year, I saw a film on television called "Garabandal, sólo Dios lo sabe" (Garabandal, only God knows). It was about the story of four girls who lived in a tiny village in Cantabria (Spain), San Sebastian de Garabandal. These girls first saw an Angel in the sky, and witnessed various apparitions of the Virgin del Carmen. On each occasion, she told them when she was going to return.

When the girls were talking to her, they became totally solid, like marble. No-one could move them. It was impossible. Also, when their dresses were pulled up a little, their feet weren't touching the ground. Many people flocked there when the girls were having these apparitions. The local Priest and the village Civil Guard, in time, really believed that this was actually happening.

However, the authorities of the Catholic Church, who were called in to study the phenomenon, didn't give any credit to these apparitions, and even tried to coax Conchita, the main "leader" and spokeswoman of the girls, to sign a document to say that she had lied.

No-one knows why the Virgin appeared to these girls in a small remote village, but the truth is, others and I believed it to be completely true. The Virgin had told them more or less the same things she had revealed to Bernadette in Lourdes, and to the three shepherds in Fatima.

The Virgin's message for all of them was that if we didn't amend our ways, and stop committing sin after sin, God would punish us for all our wrong doings. She also made it clear that she wanted Russia to be consecrated to the Sacred Heart of Mary before it was too late.

The Catholic Church revealed the first two messages that the children of Fatima gave to them, and the third one was only revealed in 1980. Now both, Lourdes and Fatima, receive millions and millions of pilgrims every year, and entire families who go there to show their faith and their love for God.

I have been to Lourdes once, and I can honestly say that it is so emotional to see people from all over the world who have so much faith and plead and pray to be healed. Even patients in hospital beds are taken into the square, where the mass is given in various languages.

On the 13th of May 1981, in St. Paul's Square in Vatican City, Mehmet Ali Agca fired four times at the Pope John Paul 11 when he entered the square. At first, it was thought that his injuries were of no importance, but he was operated on urgently for the amount of blood that he had lost.

The following year, he travelled all the way to Fatima to place in her crown one of the bullets that had injured him (it's now displayed at museum of Fatima). The Pope was convinced that the Virgin of Fatima had saved his life because the 13th of May is the date when the Virgin of Fatima appeared to three children, shepherds Lucia, Francisco and Marta, back in 1917.

Going back to Garabandal, after finding out about it, I was absolutely convinced that I had to go there. I didn't know why, but I felt that I was being drawn there for some reason. Some strange force drove me to this village, and I wanted to go as soon as possible. I had no idea what to expect, but I definitely felt I had to go.

In May 2022, a friend of mine invited me to go with her to Asturias (Spain) because she wanted to pay a tribute to

Saint Toribio in a monastery at a place called Potes, in Leibana (Cantrabia). As it was the ideal opportunity to visit San Sebastian de Garabandal, we decided to include it in our trip. I didn't think it would be easy to find, and I was very pleased we got there without getting lost. I was really excited as we were able to reach the place of the sightings by car. A Godsend, because both, her and I, have heart problems and it's very tiring to walk up steep roads.

Eventually, we got to the top and in the village we were told that we had to get to a place called "The Pines." As soon as we walked up the last path, I had butterflies in my tummy.

We went through the gate, and it was so misty we could just about see. This mist made the scene so much more intriguing. As I got close to a tree, I saw a man laying on the grass. As we got nearer, there were loads of people lying on the grass, the benches, in fact, everywhere.

There was complete silence, and you could hear a pin drop. To me, this was like the Earth meeting with Heaven. There was magic in the air. I didn't know exactly where to stand to try and speak to the Virgin, so I rested against one of my best friends, a tree.

I got all my courage up and said, "Mother, can I see you?" I got an answer immediately, telepathically that said, "No, but the fact that you have come all this way is surely proof of the great faith that you have in God." Then I asked her, "Mother, can you heal me?" And she answered, "No, that is something the Holy Ghost must do."

You can't imagine what that meant to me. I was stunned, but at the same time really chuffed. I had spoken to the Virgin Mary, me Vivienne Lee, I couldn't believe it. I felt so privileged. It was almost impossible to comprehend, but it had happened to me. I really had so much faith before I went that

I would either see or speak to the Virgin, that my dream had come true. I cried so much and felt so honoured. My prayers had been answered.

Then my friend called me over and said to me, "Hug those two pine trees over there and tell me what vibes you get."

I cuddled the first one, and I saw Jesus wearing a white tunic with a green robe over the top, like a kind of long coat or cape. He had his arms open wide, as if he was preaching.

I remembered going through the scan at Heathrow Airport, on one of my journeys back to Spain, they told me to lift my arms up and I saw myself on a crucifix.

Then I went to the second tree and cuddled it too. There I saw an image of Moses, or maybe Abraham. I saw these images so clearly.

I was told after, by a friend therapist, that the worst thing I could do was doubt about what I had heard and seen, and I must have real strong faith that the Holy Ghost is going to heal me, maybe not himself, but I could be led to someone who will.

When I told my friend what I had seen (I don't think she really believed that trees spoke to me) and she told me that when she touched the first tree it spoke to her and said "I came here over two thousand years ago to try and save humankind, but I am very disappointed with you, because in all the years that have gone by, you have learnt nothing."

It seemed to me that it was Jesus who spoke to her. She hadn't told me before I hugged the first tree what it had said to her, so really it coincided with the fact that I saw Jesus in that tree. I also wrote a poem, years before, called "The love of Jesus Christ", and in the words in it said exactly what the tree had told her, that we had learned nothing from his sacrifice. How strange?

When she touched the second tree, it told her that obviously, Jesus wasn't very happy, but at the same time not to worry, it wasn't anything to do with her. So we both had our experiences, our wonderful experiences, which I will always treasure.

35

CLOSER THAN EVER

Leaving Garabandal, I realized that I hadn't asked the Virgin if I had to do anything to gain healing from the Holy Spirit. I think that they must understand that I'm very tired after all these years of suffering, and also that I'm getting old, so I hope and pray that my wish will be granted because of my determination and bravery.

I say bravery, because I think I have done well to survive all the strange things that have happened to me without going mental, and that sometimes was extremely difficult...

One of my therapists told me that I had a dragon inside me. At the time, I was looking for answers, and I was very vulnerable, and I got to the stage where I really believed it.

I had to go to A & E and tell the doctors that I was convinced I had a dragon inside of me. Can you imagine how stupid I feel about that now? But I suppose it was part of my journey, and I was very easily influenced in those days.

Thank God, I'm OK now. I think that maybe loads of people who are in Lunatic Asylums may have had similar experiences and just couldn't cope.

Living on your own also has its pros and cons. When I had night visits and spirits calling my name, tugging on my arm or tapping me on the shoulder, I was truly and honestly scared, and had no-one to comfort me or get into bed with. You just have to get on with it and hope you won't be harmed in any way.

I only told my son about my experiences a few months ago. He had no idea of what's been happening to me over the years. I didn't want to say anything because he is terrified of all these things, mainly death, and also I didn't want him to find out via the book.

When we left "The Pines", we went into the village to buy some articles in the little shop that was there. I bought a couple of magnets for the fridge with Garabandal on them and a postcard of Conchita.

I asked the lady in the shop what had become of the girls, and she told me that three of them had gone to live in the United States and that one of them had died. The fourth one lived in that area.

I also asked her about the apparitions. She told me that the Virgin Carmen had appeared occasionally on the path that leads up to "The Pines", and that she had been accompanied by Archangel Michael.

I have a special love for Archangel Michael because about a year ago, my dear friend M. did a course of Reiki with Angels. These sessions are done at a distance, with the music she choses, and you get the picture in your mind. Right at the end of the session, Archangel Michael came to me and in old-fashioned English and said, "Don't worry I am looking over thee."

I couldn't wait to tell M. what I had seen, and she wasn't surprised, because she had summoned him before the session started. As you might imagine, I feel very close to God, each day nearer and nearer. I have never been very religious, but I took my religious classes very seriously, and above all, I was afraid of breaking any of the Ten Commandments. Why did I have this fixation? I don't know, but maybe it had something to do with a previous life.

Although most of my life, I have been suffering pain (no-one to blame). I have never given up. Im a strong old cow, just like my Mum and all my sisters and my brother. I have to admit that if all this has a positive result to help other human beings, I would gladly do it all again.

We have always been kept in the dark, one way or another, and we have believed everything that we have been taught. However, I have always kept an open mind about these things and probably nothing that could happen in the future would surprise me.

I didn't think, in a million years, I would have the possibility of talking to the Virgin, but God is nearer than we think. When you see beautiful signs, like Sun Dance, you forget about all the horrible ones. I'm relating all these things so that hopefully, in the forthcoming years, you won't be too frightened to face all the things that might happen. But remember that people like me, and other people of light, will be here to help you and convince you that if you are a good person you have nothing to fear. In my opinion, death is the beginning of a new life where you will meet up with your deceased loved ones again.

Perhaps people like me have had to pass these difficult trials and tribulations to be worthy of giving our heart and our souls to the service of anyone who is in despair or just need a shoulder to cry on.

I feel very privileged deep down, that maybe, I am one of those souls who will help when the time comes. God Willing, I will live long enough to see the changes. We are going towards a Golden Age where things will be much better (to get there, we must wake up and defend our freedom), and at long last love will overtake hate.

I wish you all a very happy future for yourselves and your families. Believe me when I say, love is the only way.

Epilogue

Savour life, enjoy it,
one thing at a time.

Kill your enemies with love.

We all have powers,
develop them to your needs.

Stand up for your rights,
fight for your freedom,
face the "global" control.

Don't be afraid of death,
get involved in the biggest
change in humankind.

Chronic pain brings on depression,
seek for healing, dance it away.

Living on earth is probably
the most difficult thing possible.
It's hard for everybody.

Be strong, my darlings, and never give up,
the light will always overcome the dark.

I love you all, dear brothers and sisters.

V. L.

Acknowledgments

I wish to thank my late husband, my son, my brother and all my sisters, especially the youngest one and close friends.

My Reiki companions, who have helped me so much in times of need and understanding. *Bendito Reiki*, as a group and through the Pandemic, we sent healing at a distance to many people with a high grade of success.

I would also like to thank J. and R. for helping me to put this book together.

1. UNANSWERED QUESTIONS 11
2. LET'S DANCE 12
3. MEETING M. 13
4. PORTUGAL 14
5. SOD'S LAW 15
6. GUARDIAN ANGEL 16
7. BROKEN PIECES 17
8. ANGELS 18
9. ETERNAL BEINGS 19
10. AND THEN CAME B. 20
11. ABOVE THE CLOUDS 21
12. B FOR BRAVERY 22
13. THE MAPLE TREE 24
14. HEALING SCARS 26
15. ENERGY 27
16. "O REI SOL" 29
17. BEING SAFE 31
18. THE UNIVERSE SPEAKING 34
19. UNDER THE SPOTLIGHT 37
20. THE KEY 39
21. HELPING OTHERS 41
22. THE BOOK 43
23. BLACKCURRANT CHEESECAKE 45
24. COME TOGETHER 47
25. BELIEVE IN MIRACLES 49
26. BEAUTIFUL EARTH 50
27. LET'S WAKE UP 52
28. REGRESSIONS 54
29. MONSTERS 56
30. LIGHTS IN THE SEA 58
31. DANCING TO LIFE 59
32. STONEHENGE 62
33. AMONG TREES 65
34. MESSAGES 67
35. CLOSER THAN EVER 72

EPILOGUE 75
ACKNOWLEDGMENTS 77

www.ingramcontent.com/pod-product-compliance
Lightning Source LLC
Chambersburg PA
CBHW050445010526
44118CB00013B/1684